However You May Wish to Interpret Me

By

Dr. Lisa R. Washington

Copyright © 2015

Dr. Lisa R. Washington

Published 2019

ISBN: 9781079004410

Cover and author photo by Brittney Samone Silver

However You May Wish to Interpret Me

The Cover

In reference to the cover, the title name was basically selected to encompass the concept of individual interpretation. From my personal perspective, the world to me appears to be more and more uncompassionate about its people's alternating personalities and characteristics of individual self. I feel the need to understand the reasoning behind its escalation of increased negative change.

I am curious to uncover or discover the cause and effects of the existence of human failure; denial of change, and the overwhelmingly obscured acknowledgement of the wonderful gifts life continues to offer mankind; especially if one attempts to acknowledge the positive aspects of life.

The topics contained within the pages of this book include God, money, politics, love, war, relationships between men and women, relationships between parent and child, death, identity, race, and the animosity amongst the differing genders. Each of these topics continues to intrigue me and influence my writing technique and style.

Being curious in nature I have been able to generate numerous topics and concepts to write about. For instance, I would observe a stranger sitting blindly as if he does not realize or know that there is a world around him waiting to be explored; a world full of unlimited possibilities and promise. Suddenly, I have compiled multiple ideas which in my opinionated observation depict this stranger as I perceived him through my own eyes.

The passion I have for understanding human behavior is of great significance to me as a writer and educator. As an observer, I am usually captivated with the ignorance of those indulging in the negative aspects of life, without fully acknowledging the consequences which are attached to their actions. Yet, I want to acknowledge, explore, and enlighten people to the dark side, and introduce them to the brighter side of life as well which many people continue to walk.

It is my personal belief that we as a society should help others replace their sense of insignificance that comes with the absence of self-value and self-worth. We must assist them in locating and recognizing the depth of their true character, their buried sense of self-esteem, their hidden acknowledgement of self-gratification, and their lack of self-respect which happens to be the foreground of self-preservation.

People should look beyond the dark and dismal shadows of life in order to witness the "wide-eyed" men, women, and children who are aching to be acknowledged. We as a society need to watch, listen, understand, and view life through their eyes. They, like so many others in the world are eager to succeed with a desiring need to survive, not only in material gain, but in the heart, mind and soul.

Therefore, we must all share with them assurance of personal acceptance of all age and race groups; as well as, socioeconomic status. As one of the most wealthy and productive societies in the world, we must assist those individuals who are struggling to acquire a positive lifestyle filled with hope and prosperity by helping them to obtain a positive and comfortable future for themselves and their families.

How you interpret the messages being conveyed in this text is based on your own views and perceptions of life. I hope you enjoy reading every poem in this book.

Biographical Note

Lisa Washington was born in Baltimore, Maryland during the cold month of November, daughter of Reginald Washington and Viola Washington. She has six living siblings. Their names are Barbara, Regina, Ralph, Roshell, David, and Chana. One sibling (Charles) died at the age of 4.

Lisa Washington was educated in Baltimore City Schools. She spent the majority of her childhood visiting family in other states learning about her heritage and family legacy. She traveled and spent months in Sunnymead and Moreno Valley, California, Delaware, and New York City. While she was being exposed to different cultures in life, her future success as an educator, writer, and mother was being cultivated through personal experiences.

She attended a series of colleges and universities in the state of Maryland. Lisa Washington graduated from Baltimore City Community College and earned an Associate of Arts Degree in General Studies. She graduated from Coppin State University earning a Bachelor of Science Degree in Criminal Justice and pursued her Masters of Science Degree in Special Education the following year. Later she attended

Loyola University in Maryland receiving a Masters of Education Degree as a Reading Specialist. Then, she obtained a Doctorate of Education Degree from Morgan State University.

Dedication

I dedicate this entire book to my "Three Brown Jewels"

Michael, Brooke, and Brittney

With all my love, respect, and

admiration…mother

Table of Contents

I Devoted My Life to You

As I awoke in the morning,

I thought of only you

While the day was passing away,

I longed to taste your dew

You were the brightest light in my day

Your powdery appearance

Had taken my breath away

When I was working,

I tried to resist your control over me

Because I was so closely drawn to you,

I could not let you be

The weakness I had for you;

It was unconditionally free

You need not had called on me;

To prove my devotion to you

For it was no wonder because

I know you knew;

Of the devoted love which I had for you

Once the day had ended and night had begun

Again I thought of only you,

For your soft white kindness

Had made me true

And once I had closed my eyes to you

I had thought of the many things

You made me do

Besides the way you have made me thirst,

In my heart, you have always come first

Before the bills

Before the wife

Before the child

Before my life

For no one and nothing

Has meant as much to me

Than your inviting white gentleness

That had set me free

For because of you that I put first

Now I lay dead within this hearse

All along I had thought

That our love was true;

As I had totally devoted my life to you

Unaware Despair

Voices creeping greatly without soul

Men walking freely and unwhole

Babies glancing at their feet

Mothers left alone without any meat

Families suffering of heart and soul

Hearts pounding greatly and bold

All asleep and unaware

Living life carelessly without despair

A People Without Unity

We have existed even before slavery

We have been separated

From our families indefinitely

Through the centuries

We have been tormented,

Abused and disgraced

We have been denied

Identification as a human race

Although we have had many

World leaders, inventors, educators,

And other famous people

During our time on earth

So many of us have died,

Been killed or re-birthed

It is sad to acknowledge

That although we have been mistreated

We refuse to stand together in unity

To avoid being defeated

Once we only had to worry about;

Being placed in bondage by another kind

Now we are being slaughtered

Within our own mines

We are not presently;

Being attacked by another kind

It is within these mines of ours

That we hear the end of our eternity

The fear of being taken away from this earth

From a people without unity

A State of Confinement

I am a man of 32 years

I am endlessly being smothered

In my own man-made fears

For 32 years,

I have been confined in this cell

My mind blocked with confusion

Leaving me in a timeless spell

I am surrounded

By bars

By four walls

And I am covered in chains

Praying daily to be

Released from my pain

Although I cannot say exactly

What has placed me here

I know I am truly one

Consumed with fear

I have broken too many laws

And I have done too many wrongs

To ever be cleared

Yet, I have managed

To consistently place myself here

Here in this confined state

A place where no one admires,

But everyone hates

An Unusual Nature

Despite the demographics most of us have,

We have continued to

Impel into destructive and deviant acts

It appears as if we have derived

Straight out of hell

Too far gone and not coherent enough

To retreat from an

Obviously dismal existence

We tend to thrive on the everyday;

Obedience of failure

Ignoring one's self-worth

Is a contributing factor

To our lack of value

Hopefully, one will capture

A blossoming dream

Unfortunately,

Hope is not a variable of possibility;

Especially when deviance

Is part of your nature

Rage

I have had ill-conceived

Thoughts of plentitude

I have expressed ambiguous

Reactions to forward utterances

Which I have perceived as being rude

Abundant in a massive bulge,

I have unlocked a hatred which

I have never indulged

Revolving constantly non- self-conceived

Invoking of jealousy, lust, and envy

Unfounded once

Released in a written page

The haste of one

Consumed entirely by rage

People of the Night

Our days are brief,

Yet our nights are long

Like vampires,

We arise strictly during the nightly hour

It is a quiet environment

Raped of glamour and song

Those who pass through this night

Are not of a tasteful breed in quality,

But are of a sour one

We constantly prey

Through the nightly hours

Briefly pausing to drink

The evening wines,

And to taste the bloody meats

Although all do not indulge

In the nightly feast

Through nightly air and visions,

Others have managed

To quench their thirst,

And feed their hunger

Once the six o'clock hour strikes,

We bow our heads

To say goodnight

Even though the nights mostly end in fright

Again we return from night to night

For our days are limited

To assure our nights

Whatever I Become

Whatever

I have endured from man

Cannot change me

However I have learned

Will not limit me

Because whatever I become,

I have derived from God

Three Brown Jewels

Three beautiful jewels

In three tones of brown

They lingeringly have

Dazzled my spirits

Innocent and pure

And glowingly with merit

They are of a rare quality

Because I have

Created them personally

They are definitely

Sentimental to me

For they are part of my entirety

There is no way in which

I could ever part from them

It would be unbearable, painful

And unjust

For they were not

Created out of lust

Instead, out of love

A rare quality

That increases their value

High above

For they are mine forever

As I am theirs

For our existence is not single,

But it is paired

For I am the rock

From which they have came

The soul part from whom

They have derived their name

Inspired

I am one inspired

By one's appreciation of life

The expectations of

Obtaining goals by strife

Consumed by my own life

I have often wondered,

Could I ever be a man's wife?

Unfair and unknown

Are life's possibilities to hype

I must allow myself to become inspired,

So I may become ripe

For my inspiration is derived

From an immortal type

The one who inspires

The Runner

Mysterious in his travels

As he passes through night into day

Extremely secretive

In his dealings with others

As he tries to make ends meet

His trusting nature

Towards his associates

Only proposes his defeat

He does not take the time

To devise his plans

Unfortunately, he quickly deals

With things at hand

Being the hidden character

Does not make him the man

Nor does it secure his future

He deludes himself and his family

By perpetrating his original character

By doing so,

He believes his intentions

To be admirable and just

Yet, how can this be

When he is being untruthful

To all of us

Lost and Gifted

A mother blessed

With skills of gold

Living life

Wild and bold

While trampling through

Life's unsuspecting doors

Her wonders of "What if"

Has been explored

Time goes on

And lets her be

Her skills of gold

Have frozen thee

The mind still wanders,

Yet the body lies there

A mother lost and gifted

Becomes but a glare

Once Loved

At last,

I have unleashed my deeply

Repressed heart

My lover has betrayed

All confidence

Which has torn us apart

Relieved,

Unknown

At this juncture in time

For my misguided beliefs

Have distorted my mind

Because lovers endure

To quest for a higher love

They make hopeful suggestions

Which incase thoughts

Unfortunate and true

Our love has ceased

No more suffering

No more grief

No more tears

A love once special

At last is at peace

Criminal and Criminality

It is a future fatality

To venture into a life

Of criminality

Maybe not within

Your reality

Unfortunately, some youths

Involve themselves

In some sort of

Criminal endeavor

It is as if they

View criminality

As their own

Personal adventure

Maybe I am simply too naïve

To believe a criminal could

Avoid selecting criminal solutions

Over conventional ones

I guess I am just an idealist

Who believes that anyone

Can overcome

Born Yet Unadorned

One enters this world

By the unity of two

One ultimately thirsts

For the blessed compassion

Of those two

One like a beggar,

Pleads for the attention

Of those who do not

Acknowledge one's existence

One like a thief in the night,

Creeps unnoticeably

To seek out what

One does not possess

When the two who have conceived

The presence of that one

Do not value nor worship their creation,

The one himself bares solely all the pain

Instead of controlling one's hurt,

One only creates conflict for oneself

For one does not know

Of any other way

To express one's sorrow

Because to be born

Completely unadorned

Only leads to one

Becoming yet scorned

A Man Who Has No Identity

My brother

I have seen you;

Therefore, I must avoid you

Like others,

I see you everyday

Because your presence is everywhere,

It is difficult for me to stay away

Through my daily travels

I see you who sit there

Waiting for nothing

Your character

Is one without substance

You need not look in the mirror,

For you have no face

You will leave this world

Suspiciously without a trace

For your life

Never really had meaning

How ashamed I am

To call you my brother

Especially when your life

Does not compare

Successfully to others

Others who have

Faces and identities

Those are the ones

Whose lives undoubtedly

Hold true meaning

The Misery of a Man

Why does a man

Choose to wallow

In his own misery,

Especially when he has

No reason to be

A man mentally

Alone in the world

One who has

Forsaken his children,

His own life,

And that special girl

A man who once

Had what other men

Only dreamt of having

The perfect children

The perfect world

The perfect wife

Yet, he turned his back

On what once was

His kingdom

To roam in a world

Without meaning

A world of ugliness

Sorrow, and pain

A world in which

One only loses, not gain

A world in which only

The dark side appears

This world was once

Non-existent in his life,

But now it is near

It appears not only

In the physical sense

Of existing, but it exists

For him mentally

And emotionally as

He allows it to

This is not

The allowance of a man,

But it is truly

The allowance of a fool

Going Nowhere

I have skipped a block

I have walked a mile

I have run a marathon

Yet I have never seen the Nile

He Who Once Was My Father

He frequents me

In my dreams,

Occasionally, when

I feel afraid and alone

He visits me

When he comes to me

In my dreams,

I feel a sense

Of happiness and joy

He makes me feel as if

Everything is as it once was

Secure, safe, and somber

Whenever he visits me

In my dreams,

I feel secure and complete

I have no need to fear

Nor to weep

Because I know

He is within a night's reach

I can sleep

Without worrying about tomorrow

I feel sincere happiness

Not sorrow

For I am certain that one day

When I am

Completely secure and strong

I know he will come no more

For that will be the day

When I will close that

Door of loneliness

And I shall weep no more

Sheer Ignorance

Stupidity

Unfair

Unfair is typical

Considering

One is born poor

Unfair is reasonable

Being one is refused

The opportunity

To obtain wealth

Unfair is non-blasé

When we are

Supposedly entitled

To due process

Unfair is a silent cry

Of utterances by

Non-educated

Non-privileged people

Unfair is considered

An abated issue

When stated too often

The Pain of Living and the Pleasure of Death

Oh Lord, I have been

At your front door twice before

I have seen

The beauty of your home,

And I have seen

The welcoming light

That guided me to you

My Lord, I have

Tried to live my life

According to your word

Lord, I have tried

To cleanse my soul and my heart

Completely for me

To be worthy

Of receiving your blessings

Yet, I have failed continuously

Oh Lord, I pray

Credit

Credit this

Credit that

Manufacturing

Credit card debt

Consumers beware

Creditors

Are not fair

Consumers ending up

On welfare

No money for food

No money for clothes

Backed up on bills

Avoiding phone calls

Necessity

Want

Necessity

Need

Please!

Define the situation clearly

Is this a want?

Or is this a need?

Consumer beware

Consumer beware

Of your own

Personal greed

Turn Off the Light

Leave the room dark

Play no tunes

Play no shows

Block the light of the moon

Whisper in breath

Speak no lines

Remain in your area

I will remain in mine

Light no candle

Flash no light

No need for food

No need for drink

No need for blankets

No need to think

Say no prayer

Spark no flame

Just say "Goodnight"

Goodnight, Goodnight

My body will not twitch

I will night fight

Please! Just turn off the light

Truth or Dare

I don't care if you stare

I won't move if you swoon

I don't lie when you laugh

I won't complain about being last

I didn't run when you joked

I wouldn't smoke when you offered

I just pretended to

Mother May I

Mother may I

Mother may I speak

My tongue has grown legs

And has run away from me

Mother may I look

My eyes have rolled backward repeatedly

Mother may I listen

My ears have closed off to sound

Mother may I sing

My voice has ceased with song

Mother may I stand

My feet have sprouted wings

And flown away

Mother may I learn

My mind is consumed with questions

Mother may I live

My life has been infringed upon

By your personal needs

Mother may I leave

I need to taste the world

As there still exists

A being in my body

Mother may I

Sister, Sister

Sister, sister

Stop your crying,

Stop your lying

Sister dear,

I know you

Are not trying

You have been

Complaining for years

Releasing your fake tears,

Causing massive floods

Falsifying love

Creating misery and pain,

Assuming fame

Where there is no reign

Sister, sister

I must lay down the law

Sister, you are

Indeed, living raw

Do you fear the end?

Sister do you even care?

Sister, sister

Countdown

Ten: Presumptions of security

Nine: Glamorizing and polarizing

      our nationally known cities

Eight: Sleeping with world known enemies

Seven: Exposing ourselves to modern day

      technology

Six: Becoming overly ambitious by

      exaggerating our power

Five: Assuming an ultimate invincibility

Four: Forgetting to calculate possible

      fatalities

Three: Embracing all whom come across

      our great seas

Two: Neglecting our nation, its people,

      and their civil liberties

One: September 11th, the destruction took

flight on the land of the free

Zero: Never again will be so naive

Reality

We are born

We struggle

We adjust

To life's troubles

We repeat

Each of our mistakes

We mingle

In each other's race

We tempt fate

By rushing in life

We usually experience

Everything twice

Love

Children

Relationships

Careers

We create a legacy

We develop fame

We do all these things

In leaving our names

We then travel

Through the hourglass

As we slide through

The tainted glass

Our minds begin to clutter

Our memories

Become impaired

Our vision

Gradually gets distorted

Reality becomes the final stage

Life

Racing through a straight tunnel

Looking for light

Announced as being the winner

Of a close race

Advancing fast

To qualify for first place

Ducking and dodging

Multiple bullets

It is a miracle

I am here

The race has started again

Infancy

Toddlerhood

Childhood

Adolescence

Adulthood

Then, I cease to exist

Death

Death is the end of life,

The state of being dead

Destruction

Extinction

Slaughter

Epitaph is the inscription

Of memory I have of my brother

Still

Alone

Cold

Frail

Alarming is my knowledge of death

Untimely

Random

Non-prejudicial

Tragic are my thoughts

About death as it stains my heart

Reaching out to grab its victims

Lamentable

Unfortunate

Horrifying is the concept

Of its power and its ability to alter life

To Castrate

To Change

To Spay

Death means to cease to exist

Death means to fade away

Life, Death, and Circumstance

There is more to life

Than material gain

Emotions filled with torment

Definitely

Life guarantees no gain

Nor does it promise reign

Knowing that the

"American Pride"

Is a controversial thought

I am however non-partisan

In respect to that part

This "American Dream"

In which I have

Is both valuable and priceless

Indeed, I say

I wish to leave a legacy

For my children's children

Yet, I am uncertain when

My journey may end

I feel I have the ability

To continue in life

I feel I can

Move forward in strife

This is my life

And I have yet to obtain

My ultimate dream

Due to life, death, and circumstance

Based on a timeless theme

Coppin State College

You have a reputation

For housing some of the most

Affluent, dedicated, and

Educated men and women

You conjure up

Individual excellence,

Perfection and patience

According to your children

You are both mother and father

To many even though you dictate

How to do

How to master

How to evolve

You frequently

Issue statements of

Facts

Current Events

Substance

For me, you will

Always represent so much

In which I may never live up to

Honor

Respect

Historical and Monumental Empowerment

You have provided me with opportunities

Where once there was doubt

You challenged me

To prove myself to you

You have set high expectations

For me to achieve

You have given me no sympathy

You forced me to think

You allowed me to dream

You have given nothing away for free

You have called on me

To demonstrate my ability to succeed

You were there for me

When my life seemed unsure

You grabbed my hand

And you escorted me through the door

You allowed me to explore everything

I could have even imagined

You are Coppin State College

Pride

Prestige

Prosperity

And Excellence

Decompression

Standing alone in a sealed room

I stand quietly still

Waiting for my limbs to bloom

Conflicting thoughts

Passing through my mind

The air is extremely thin

Oxygen begins to evacuate my lungs

Suction pulling on my frail bones

My veins are crawling,

And they are breathing rapidly

The moisture has dried from my juicy lips

My once smooth skin

Is covered with cuts, burns and rips

What kind of freaked out trip is this?

The Unruly Ones

Two degrees of desperation

Diligent psyche

Confused nations

Thoughts of plentitude

Individualized, grouped, or paired

Known for being rude

Blatant accusations being made

Frustrated, anxious, driven thoughts

Immortal ideas transpired from grade

Consumed with contempt

In my masked heart

Of no commonality with peers

Kisses full, convincing and dart

The mind is its own tainted chamber

Usually free of spirit

Recently guided by anger

Ruthless in mind

Free of guilt

Vengeful character wrapped in vine

Deadly, unsuitably disrespectful fun

The privilege of being considered

One of the unruly ones

Dr. King

Dear Dr. King,

I have always valued your dream

I believe you have made a major impact

On your people's dreams

You have encouraged us all too dream

Children are now able to sing

Because of you, who held a sacred truth

My children can sing various songs

Their abilities stretch

From America to Rome

At Last

At last…

At last I am free

At last…

At last I am committed to no one

At last…

At last I have no dependents

At last…

At last I am my only concern

At last…

At last I come and go as I please

At last…

At last I must answer to no one

At last…

At last I am alleviated of financial burdens

At last…

At last I am the only one to focus on

At last...

At last I am me

Miss Understood

You have called me out

Of my name repeatedly

Ms. Jealous Doe

Ms. High-Sedate Slick

Ms. Show-Off Jones

Ms. Stuck-Up Smith

Ms., She Thinks She's Better than

Everyone Else Evens

You have been adamant

With each of your utterances

Ms. Thing

Ms. This

Ms. That

Ms. Thought She Was All About That Black

You might NOT acknowledge

Who I am, but I can

I am MISS UNDERSTOOD

People of Obscurity

We hide in a closet

We live ten to a house

We wear gruesome masks

We have multiple names

Yo

Homie

Bro

We sometimes house in boxes

We are different people

We live to play games

The mask I wear is

Covered with sequence

Dripping in jewels

Laced with the rarest of materials

Like an Egyptian Princess my skin is

Blanketed with expensive oils

Enriched with creams

Painted with colored powders

My body is immersed in jasmine and lilac

My body is cleansed and fresh

I make rich my skin

External satisfaction

No internal metamorphic change

Black reign

Black skin

Black pain

Troubled times

No sunshine when we are gone

No signs of life when we refuse to live

No respect for each other

When we refuse to love

No sense of urgency

When we witness murder

No will to repent

When we cause hurt and harm

No reason to speak out

When we hear hateful words

No clue to how this institution

Of life is being ridiculed

No intention on making changes

No one wants to take a stand

No one cares to provide resolve

No one really wants to see the truth;

No one wants to acknowledge

These troubled times

War Games

The trudging of soldiers' boots

Stomping on the ground

Each step moving towards the river

The agony of the sound

A hollow ground with bodies dead

Lying all around

An unspoken grief left in peace

The thought of the fallen at my feet

Grenades and riffles weapons of choice

The metal antiquities

Manmade arsenals of war

A military exercise like never before

Tactical impressions

Forced and assertive aggression

Battle maneuvers arguably stretched

A bland and complex picture forever etched

The Air force, Army, Navy, Marines

Figures of military forces which beam

Ideals of solidarity beliefs

And brotherly pride

Voices which harbor a strong unbidden tide

Spontaneous, unprompted, voluntary acts

An unwavering resolve

Military tactics at best

The living breath of war games

America

With the earliest rays of the sun

Comes a dimmer of light

Like the Sumerians, America

Has ruins of ancient times

Civilization is her history

A conundrum

Her words; the equivalent

Of a striking force against a rock;

A mighty blow controlling this great temple

Does not protect the villagers

City, state, country continues

To fight among themselves

This realm of embodiment

A crested link to civilization

On the brink of destruction

Alluded to meet a preconceived catastrophe

America once admired and loved

The Student

Sitting in the classroom;

Not present to be absent

Intellectual ability measured quantitatively;

On a staunch April day

The teacher stands before them

With authoritative appeal

A mutual sense of respect;

Illuminating in the room

Anticipation awaiting every girl and boy

It emerges in their voices;

A collective sound which may annoy

Thoughtfulness in a delivered ploy

They wait for direction

And engage in discussion

Blatantly; they often

Deviate from instruction

Not an alien abduction, but a lack of will

Diverge, digress, depart, and stray

Students ignoring the significance in grades

Gwendolyn Brooks;

Raptures of education at bay

A clear day begins to fade away;

Especially when learning

Is not valued from day to day

Teacher

Release your knowledge to me

Educate my earthly being;

Multiple intelligences arise

Within my innocent eyes

Polarized by words alone

A life I must condone

Intellect known to thee

A Call for Peace

Today I call for peace;

Peaceful protest

Peaceful resolve

The peaceful actions

Of all involved

The Year of the Kill

Philosophical Bullets penetrating the air

Chamber emptied;

Victims spread across the sea

Anger exhorting numerically

Citizens divided from shore to shore;

Imminent dangers abound;

A sweeping wave of hostility

The brewing wind looming off the coast

Archaic actions bestowed on these plains

Menacing, expected gaze of current days

Boundless and plentiful deaths

Comparative to past wars

Wars of the Roses

Wars of Alexander the Great

Wars of the Sixteen Kingdoms

Wars without faith

Medieval, primitive, archaic stance

Crusade or conquest a matter of opinion

Manmade ideals of personal dominion

Antiquated rituals of man

Death Tolls

A devastating reality for humanity

Death toll rising; people dying senselessly

A mockery to life, the pursuit

Of happiness and liberty

Ignoring the hope;

The American Dream tarnished

Thirty Seconds to Mars;

The Kill

The judgment

Prudence, Wisdom, and Perception

Knocking at my door

The judgment call to take the fall,

For all cast to Hell

And once I acknowledged the acuity

Of our limitless sins

Marching forward towards the light

My journey begins to end

A Matter of Seconds

Seconds disappear in a heartbeat

A Twinkling moment in time

Half a second has passed;

Between your life and mine

A fraction of a minute

The blink of an eye

Instantly gone

The day in which I die

Distorted Truth

Truths can be easily distorted,

Between people of all colors;

Lies characteristically manifested over time

Within this quiet place of detachment;

Distorted truths which exaggerate

And twist reality

Scholastic abilities confirmed;

Complex and surreal

Demoralizing to those who feel its wrath;

Over-arching real-world problems,

Lacking sharply in quality

And overall appeal

Imparting knowledge; bringing forth change

A simple truth beyond the present

Defeatist attitudes emerging

Among black youth

The harshest of all truths

Contemplating a dismal reality of our youth;

Self-doubt flourishing within our mines

No pressure to stay in school;

Under minded confidence

In a corrupt system

Our ability challenged at every aspect in life

Facilitation of heart and soul

Grasping one's last breath to stand bold;

Probing and prodding to seek

An unspoken truth

Intellectual evaluation of the black youth,

ACT, SAT, standardized tests;

An innocent soul not yet at rest

Black achievers

Black professionals and believers;

Blacks living prosperous middle-class lives

Poisonous stereotypes projected

In movies and media; intellectually adept

To current America doubts harbored

The Nationalist

Belief in country is proudest

When Patriotisms alive

Voices echo loudest in the blue open sky

People stand rejoicing

As the crowd passes by

Loyalty to country

Emphasizes why

Obligation to nation stands tall

Allegiance to a country

That will never fall

Pride and dignity; to the extreme

Desire to understand what it truly means

To be an American of this great land

A peaceful breath from the working man

We the People

We the people

Of this great nation

Promise to restore

Order in our government

To reunite the citizens

Of America in brotherhood

Provide equal justice

Under the law for all men

To protect this country and its people

Promote love, peace and happiness

Establish a common ground

Trumpism

A collective loss of cohesion and control

Based upon one's inflated ego

Conclude not your own beliefs

Blanketing America in lies and deceit

Tell me briefly about Russian spies

In an attempt to set my mind at ease

Tweet me twice to dismiss collusion

Alleviate all aspects of national confusion

Become better at critiquing your words

Your racial connotations are inflammatory

An unflattering example

Of a never-ending story

Be steadfast in your leadership approach

Rawness, hardness, and credibility

Historical traits of a true presidency

Resort to acts which constitute Patriotism

Consume the human spirit

Cynical Political calculations bare no merit

Avoid inciting episodes of racism

Celebrating profits of cynicism

An eventual confinement

Every step closer to darkness

Community stability breaking down

Conspired actions of an unworthy crown

A casualty of diplomacy a political unrest

This is Trumpism at its best

A Nation at War

Warred against my enemy

Bothered by my foe

A nation at war from long ago

Promises of unity seasoned in hope

Combating differences once remote

A staunch memory of the Civil War

Vendetta or military action explored

Hostilities of Napoleonic wars

A minor infraction of warfare

Usual Suspects

Perpetrators of abandonment

Children left alone

Echoes of silence

In this shattered home

Pawns in a game that no one wins

The lions share their prey

In a hollow din

The mating dance repeated

Intertwined destiny and love

Bound to each other

Like two gliding doves

Morality lecturers

For a spell

Trying to remind me

Of my manmade Hell

The Darkest of Days

I wish that the darkest of days

Would quickly fade away;

If not for current reality

These tragic events would not be;

A marginal glitch in our lives

In the ocean these things thrive;

Resurfacing quickly from the sea

To broker doubts inside of thee

A longing once buried deep

That overtook my quiet sleep;

Existing in my darkest dreams

Mournful thoughts of Elegy

In the Name of Peace

I plead the fifth to shelter my soul

Confining thoughts to the world below,

When summer comes, I shield my eyes

Preventing myself from spreading lies;

And when in doubt I cling to peace

A human action that releases me

While towering walls

No words will leap

Keeping restraint

To ensure an earthly peace

Mount Sinai as the beacon of hope;

Urges me to pledge this oath

Race Relations

O' Be it Hostile words of Envy

Cased in seeds of gold

The beliefs of man are planted

Which strike a mighty blow

In my adult brain I question

All that I can see

The Old South standing right in front of me

Painfully tangible memories of brutality

Executions which spoke volumes

In our History

Regarding the value of Black life

I often contemplate

Justification of actions built solely on Hate

Extinguishing the violence from current day

Requires true devotion of Unity

Alienated hearts of the possessed may speak

A system which breads resentment

Deep inside of me

Black men rising out of the ash and flames

Enthralled in revolutionary rhetoric

Echoed through their human pain

A rap song so spiteful; repetitive and true

Speaking truth to power

That we already knew

Self-delusion a costly expense

Which we cannot afford

Interpretations of race relations

Generally ignored

Reality Unhinged

Mind! You will drift away!

The id, the ego, and the superego

Even though you will forget

The knowledge I have gave

I refuse to let you fade away

When memory loss

Claims your thoughts

Come back to me again;

So, I can revive your conscious thoughts

Of whom you were back then

The Abandoned Dreamers

Petrified wood rooting

Deep in the wilderness,

The core of its shell hollow and vacant

The soul of the wood scattered on the ground

Evidence of heart never to be found

Disputes of purpose unseen

Unrequited roots of its form

The possibility of life never born

Deteriorating along a quiet stream

A Saint in the City

On the streets of this cold, dark city

Bullets fly day and night

Innocent children; canonized

Reflective images of angels

Hovering high above

Countering these deadly slugs

A saintly vision of spectacle

Holy-virtuous saintly acts of love

Capsulated in a dream

In the Dead of Night

When the dark of the world rest in me

I lie down under the tree of empathy

For a moment I rest in time

To quantify the images in my mind

Routine dilemma or difficulty

A broken promise of history

Declaration of truth and guarantee

Bountiful broken branches

Deep into this dark night

The dead are residing

An echo of a shallow tomb

Illuminating in this dark and dismal gloom

Down the Road of Life

While walking through the road of life,

I stumbled over my past

A tragic scene of destiny standing in the road

But, daylight comes and I walk on

And suddenly I see

A brand-new world of possibilities

Right in front of me

Yet, I fear each step

As I go further down the road

Too frighten to comprehend

The things which I must let go

Democrats and Republicans

Advocates and supporters of truth

Representatives of citizen groups

An ambient political party

Believers of equality or not

A preordained conspiracy plot

Prescribed fate-doom or destiny

Forms of government

Belonging to the republic

Raging wars of diplomacy

Disparaging acts of disagreements

Political foes; derogatory woes

Built entirely on corrupted egos

Or not

A Woman's Choice

Reflecting on days long gone

I stumble by the neighbors' pond

Looking at frogs and tadpoles leap

I fall into a timeless sleep

An hour later a man calls

We walk towards the waterfall

Briskly walking step by step

I gasp for a second breath

Before my eyes

I see a ring

A diamond bright

Glittering green

I ponder to say yes or no

Behooving to me; I lose my voice

The true pressure of

A woman's choice

The Deep Blue Sea

Bordering on our greatest divide

An ocean strong, deep, and wide

Greece, Turkey, and Libya too

Focused on the ocean blue

Currents came upon the sea

A drifting mass of water breeze

The steady flow and upward draft

An electrical essence from the past

Twere upon this evening of midnight blue

A Mediterranean Sea renewed

A cold, wet climate has been unleashed

Weathering conditions prevail

A calming peace

Night

As soon as day begins,

The darkest hour comes

Dragging deep into the night,

A raging gorging sum

I look up at the sky,

The stars begin to gleam

Behold

My questionable eyes

See a glowing sea

Perplexing how

My thoughts

Of night may seem

The Good Fight

He charged the opposition

With brief and timely submission

His strategic plan sours

Then re-engaged himself into flight

Within a single hour

His manly means blew quickly

Moving like a Bolt his essence;

A man of strength and dignity

His body firm against

The plank of prosperity

Betrayal

Putting others in front of us

Unjustifiable inklings of lust

Disloyalty- treachery- perfidy

Lacking in partnership and unity

A bad faith oath of duplicity

Deception- treason- a breach of faith

Double- dealing Judas

Divulgence of secrets

Of our government crest

Leaking and telling of information

A cowardly act of a broken man

Built on faithlessness appeal

A true discourse of political betrayal

A Guilty Man

Culpable killer

Locked in a vault

Criminal- sinful-

Unforgiveable thoughts

Incarcerated and shamed

On social media

Blameworthy like those

Listed in the encyclopedia

Hitler, Bundy, Dahmer,

Gacy- blamable wrong-doers

At fault; at will

Without second thought

Responsible for unspeakable evils

Answerable to the jury;

Twelve sitting still

Accountable for his actions

Liable for repel

Assault and battery

Possible charges applied

Reprehensible- felonious-

Delinquent actions

Of a guilty and crazed man

Convicted on the judicial stand

A Life of War and Words

In this world of war and words

The fetal lamb is led to slaughter;

Husbands- wives- sons- daughters

The black sheep put out to pasture

A refuge of organic matter;

Continual change leaping over death

The existence of being among the living

An innocent soul laid to rest;

Survival of the fittest a general ease

Viability- survival- a human entity

Mortal is the soul captured in a shell

A captivating image of a timeless spell

Creation from God; father of Abraham

The state of confusion at bay

The origins of a human being

Quietly and neatly tucked away

Personal Reflection

While my mind was unwinding;

Problems invaded my thoughts

A massive and colossal scheme

Rebuking past midnight dreams

I reflect on my rapid memories,

My mind a memory bank

Depositing every encounter

Of future and past mistakes

Inspiration

Things that inspire me

Dreams-Hopes-Love-Family

All of which encourage me

Other things which represent me

Assertiveness- Will- Integrity

All of which leads to prosperity

The remaining truths which guide my path

My three children who make me laugh

Michael- Brooke- Brittney

My true inspiration

Professional Suicide

Accepting falsified comments

And entangled facts

Realizing how authority

Stabs us in the back

Ignoring signs of corruption in sight

Indulging in conversations

Based on falsehoods

Misconceptions of facts

And absence of truth

Refusing to see

What is in front of you

The cold hard facts

Staring you in the eye

Questionable actions

Of the other guy

A colleague, an administrator,

An ignorant man

Someone who lies

And pretends to be your friend

Be mindful of things

Which emerge within your base

The solitude of existing

Not in this falsified place

A space confined by a system of doubt

Realities of truths never come to light

Despite one's intention

To acknowledge what is right

A hard look at things

Which emerge from hate

An unrealistic look

At another man's fate

A state of confusion

A state of self loathing

A state of a man

In danger of imploding;

Deep within the bows

Of a shallow tomb

Coated in jealously,

Hate, and envy loom;

Recognition of truth;

Recognition of being

A miniature scope

Of a collective scene

Elements of grief

And verbal messages of sting;

People camouflaged

As human beings

Those who participate

In professional suicide

Often question themselves

And wonder; why?

The Unprofessional

The epitome of cruel

An unethical human being

Someone new on the work scene;

An invader of sorts

A despicable person;

Someone consumed with hate

A true unprofessional

The Model Teacher

Someone who speculates

On every aspect of an instructional path

Someone who looks for perfection

Which often briefly lasts?

From day to day performance;

Of whimsical appeal

Rotation of effective strategies

Encased in a model lesson;

Of rigor and complexity

The Darkest Hour

Bring fourth the light in a glass

Bestow a hope expected to last

Part the darkness with a knife

Bridge your life to this day

Speak of plans of future dreams

Tell me exactly what this means

A quiet breath of shallow ease

Deeply engaged in the breeze

Propose your faith into this world

Reject temptation from a girl

Lust is just a brief quake

The darkest hour of your mistake

The Devil Within

This is the reality which all men reap

A time of judgment we often repeat

The reality of the current world

These are the years some will regret

Taking chances to win a losing bet

No chance of living a decent life

On a dark and dreary day,

The devil comes out to play

A thunderous roar

Engulfs the gray and looming day

Men will not acknowledge

Their individual mistakes

This is the time to make peace

Within your soul

Retribution of one's

Inflated ego must let go

Time to release

The devil within you

A Body of Four

A collective group of human beings

Silently walking down, a stream

The water is quiet

And running smooth

Deep within a hollow tube

Projected images of things to come

Reflecting on the days of Rome

Traveling through life's

Unexpected doors

My wondering of my

Future has been explored

A settle breath released within

Projecting evidence

Of a thorough win

Stepping silently

At a constant pace

An internal peace

Which has been erased

Images of truths

Can spill regret

The ocean wide

And stretched abound

The four of us living

In this remote town

An unexpected

Turn of events

A Burning Peace

A flicker of raging red fire;

Burning deep within my head

Buried six feet within my mind

Latent thoughts from another time

Projected images from the past;

A burning peace I laid to rest

Ten years ago, due to circumstance;

Too troubling to reveal in the light of day;

A hidden darkness never to be released

A burning peace inside of me

A Girl's Dreams

The light shines

Brightly in the sky

Reflecting upon her

Delicate human form

Images of innocence

Tip-toe across the fields

Pacing her every move

As she wonders through the plain

Stretching and reaching

Across the great hills

While the world watches her grow

And sunshine glistens

In her earthly eyes

A beautiful star has

Awakened in the universe

The internal self

Has emerged from within

Her calm nature

Evokes the coming dawn

A girl's dreams

Have been reborn

Unmasking

The true character of self

The Cold War

Frigid, lonely, desperate unnerving

Natural elements experienced in war

A tension great and unexpected

1947 through 1991

An extension of a previous one

Restricted rivalries emerged

Countries bound to battle serge

Descriptive political and economic stance

Propaganda lacking a united romance

The discourse between a limited few

Bordering on World War II

Recourse to weapons abound

A bloody massacre on common ground

American Retreat

The passage to America can be treacherous

Crossing the deep and dangerous waves,

Driving through the daunting roads,

Or making passage across the friendly skies

Regardless of your plight,

The destiny is certain

A brisk and refreshing end

To a challenging journey,

The final destination

Of solitude and sanctuary

A common retreat many

Have ventured in the past

Living in America

Breathing, eating, loving,

And lusting for life

Faced with multiple adversities;

The reality of what has always been

A brief utterance from a childhood friend

Eager to embrace what life has to offer

Opportunity abounds

On this common ground,

Ready for any challenge which springs

Embarking on manmade American Dreams

Remembering the past

As I look towards the future;

Discovering what others have uncovered

The stealth reality of American lovers

In an awkward and thrusting push

Searching for something that was not there;

Closeted in a shadow of an unearthly glare

An embodiment of rare images

Cloaked in a dismal

And enchanting dream

Far reaching from my human hands

I am predisposed by what I see

Incapable of acknowledging

My own dreams;

Condemned by this truth

The Unspoken War

We hint to how the soldiers played

Watched as they embraced their day

Weathering nights of dark dreams

Winter is never a welcoming scene

Waiting for a silent storm of peace

Whatever I think I give to thee

Wanting to pose a phrase to see

Why did they cross that path?

Wishing to avoid God's holy wrath

Wondering if my quiet voice can be heard

Without singing like a hummingbird

Wanting desperately to reveal

The secret at bay

Tales of Life

I listen closely to the tales of life

To walk beside my distant wife

Protecting my heart, I often lie

While projecting a childhood lullaby

I convince myself that this is my fate

Launching my thoughts into outer space

For a brief moment in time I often wonder

The gravity of the spell I am presently under

Remnants of reality or fantasy;

As we stroll hand and hand along the sea

Who is this person traveling at my side?

Memories of my lovely childhood bride

Raw: War in Reverse

Forming alliances

And building hope

Breaking boundaries

Which have divided us

Creating relationships

Built solely on trust

Establishing a union

For all to benefit

Understanding that men

Can be friends

Promoting a truce

To remain united

Realizing that

Our common beliefs

Are intertwined

Bridging new memories

For historical observations

Making national

And international anew

Trying to enforce

Policies which promote life

Being steadfast

In our democratic approach

Appreciating each other

For our uniqueness

Embracing all we have

To contribute to life

Contemplating wholeness

For all men

Uniting under a colorful

And common flag

Raw are the ideals

Of war in reverse

Messages from Above

Looking upon a midnight star

I listen for a message far

Beneath the heavens within the blue

An inkling of hope becomes anew

Hesitant to embrace the whispering voice

Acknowledging that I have no choice

To comprehend the messages from above

A quiet voice which speaks of love

Twice I heard the speaker speak

Reminding me to spread love and peace

Captivated by the sound of angels all around;

On the edge of this quiet and remote town

The Human Spirit

Deep within the soul of thee,

Thou strength and honor exposed

Twere not for the brief image of me

I shall never, ever truly know

Who thou have placed in my shell

Bountiful memories of a single Hell

Trapped within the Ark of Noah

Referencing lines from Adam and Eve

Capturing the human spirit of thee

The brutal truth of this endless story

An obvious and jealous allegory

Rearranging Cain and Abel's truth

Reflecting on the human spirit

An overwhelming speculation of youth

An age-old belief of natural merit

Conjuring up thou belief in me

Post War Tragedy

Skeptic of the mental mind

Metaphysics of a daunting kind

Reflections of death and blood abound

Soldiers falling on the battle ground

A disturbing truth between these walls

Together we stand, divided we will fall

The greatest of battles since Normandy

The crushing post war tragedy

Combatants to the Axis Powers

Thirsty for answers at this hour

Limited resource and military powers

Embarking on our darkest hour

Rejection

Dismissed instantly

Refused acknowledgement

Absence of proposal

Denial of entry in the realm

Sheer abandonment

Dismissal of identity

Desertion from the infantry

Turned down at every turn

Avoidance cutting dead

Rejected voices in my head

Dislocation of my place

Ostracizing having grace

Knocked-back several years

Memories accompanied by tears

Shouldering grief inside of me

Devastating as it seems

Repudiation in a dream

Exclusion and avoidance

Turned down by many voices

Excommunication abounds

Absolution

Releasing myself of formal shame

I pledge to restore my given name

Be it guilt, obligation, or punishment

I know this I shall repent

Forgiveness is what I hope to receive

Indulgence, hope, and mercy

Exoneration from my past

Contained within this hourglass

An echoed truth of amnesty

Contained within this human being

Freedom and liberty releases me

Deliverance towards a brief reprieve

A Question of Morality

I often question the acts I indulge

The good, the bad, and the evil ones

Questioning ethics of right and wrong

Virtue and goodness escaped

Morality built solely on haste

Uprightness towards righteousness

Purity wrapped in wedding bliss

Decency and probity forced away from me

Blamelessness a sharp decline of morality

These are things I hope others will not see

A Matter of True Circumstance

Born into this world alone

Restricted from returning home

Long gone from my mother's watch

Forced to survive on my own ability

Unaware of how difficult it would be

Yet, managed to brace the weathering storm

The challenging reality of being born

Humble am I to say the least

Embracing the shore of life with ease

Remembering what has brought me here

A pinnacle of truth on the highest peak

The will encased within my being

The crowning point; the zenith of hope

A refusal to ever let my dreams go

The haunting past I keep contained

A summit point of sheer daunting pain

Miraculous this journey has been

Perfection on a timeless whim

Climax and vertex sitting on the shelf

Representing descriptions

Of my intuitive self

A person full of hope and pride

Emergence of strength housed deep inside

Ascendancy contained within

Propelled me into this current win

A woman of substance; a woman of grace

Traveling in this earthly place

Reaching for the mountaintop

Refusing to let go or ever stop

Limitless dreams; limitless strength

Embracing my current circumstance

Cellular Minds

People embrace technology,

Escaping reality as human beings

Besieged by an immediate response

Their intellectual minds have moved on

Towards the realm of destiny

Away from the human scene

A remote state of mind

Cellular equipped in a technical bond

Streaming on an electrical beam

Images of an absent human being

Cryptic Messages

A message written in invisible ink

Often makes a person think;

Of codes and acronyms, they once knew

Deciphering what is being said to you

An unclear and hidden quote

A secret statement on a note

Paper crisp, white and new

Presented right in front of you

An actual phrase or word exposed

Straightforward message enclosed

Within the seams of the note

Cryptic messages remain untold

Who am I

People attempt to question me

As if they do not see a human being

A person standing in front of their face

Someone of another race

Direct am I to speak my mind

Historical remnants of another kind

Too short to grasp the open sky

Too tall to explain the reasons why

Who am I? You may ask

I am someone from the past

From the days of Moses

From the days of Kings

I am what you are

I am a human being

The Bitter Truth

Sour are the words I spoke

Contained within a hidden joke

Verbal expressions of humor employed

Not intended to harm or destroy

Cautious are the words I say

Being mindful of the current day

A time of skepticism and pain

Preventing me from releasing my reign

Reflecting deeply on the words I spoke

Wishing they could be revoked

A quick silence all aloof

This is just the bitter truth

Dormant

Sleeping in a transient state

I struggle effortlessly to stay awake,

Leaving nothing behind but a dark dream

Wondering how this all may seem

Slumbering and resting on my bed

Latent resemblance of the dead

Quake the motionless of my being

Inactive, sluggish, and immobile

Comatose for a brief while

Stagnant and lethargic

A practical human trick

Suspended physical function

The Month of November

The eleventh month of the year

Echoing in the hemisphere;

Too cold to take a summer walk

A time when winter will embark;

Grasping at our fingers and feet

A time when some concede defeat;

Challenging times for those who rule

Competition between the two of you

Dressed in red and dressed in blue

The last month of autumn anew

Neighbors

Chatting in the summer breeze

Embracing the brief subtlety

Triggering thoughts of solitude

Mentioning events of being rude

Sprinting down the hill I see

A quiet voice to the left of me

Gleaming with the brightest smile

Neighborly friends all the while

Parenthood

Responsibility a needed trait

Raising children in good faith

No one questions my ability

Being a person of dignity

Childhood

Tiny footsteps running across the floor

Eyes peeking through an opened door

An abundance of toys in a box

Little feet in brand new socks

Innocence and love an internal truth

Derived from the two of you

Mother and father singing songs

Devoted daily to the little ones

Perfection not a common thread

Engrained within a parent's head

Too young to work; too young to drive

Embracing one's childhood pride

A Personal Choice

I approached a stranger I did not know,

Surfing the waves of my superego

Abrupt in conversation in toe

A situation from long ago

He looked upon my face and said,

Hello with a subtle seamless dread

Confused by my direct quote;

The stranger released his own ego

The moment I knew he had no choice

I fell into a lonely and hollow voice

Captivated by the sense of intrigue;

I wondered of what this life could mean

Too naïve to evaluate this scene;

I stumbled loudly upon the stream

Regaining my balance immediately

The Substitute

Replacement for the other guy

No one ever questions why

An alternative choice

A fill-in with a unique voice

The understudy in a Broadway show

Surrogate to my mother; Flow

Deputy to a biological brother

Standby, step-in reserved for one

Preference to replace another

An exchange, switch or trade

The original will surely fade away

The Dark Room

Isolated from the rest of the house

Too frightening for a little mouse;

Deep within a narrowing hall

The light is absent where the darkness falls;

Clinking sounds echo in the dark

Leading to this internal spark;

Upon the door my innocent eyes fall

Hidden secrets beyond these walls

Illuminating in the air

A ghostly figure near the stair;

Repeatedly avoiding that hidden room

Creeping upon a midnight doom

Honesty at Bay

Integrity and morality ignoring fear

Principles of truth we all hold dear

The crippling sound of vitality

Goodness, virtue and fidelity

At safe distance thoughts of honesty awaits

Genuineness and outspokenness contemplate

At arms length sincerity is embraced

Honesty at bay in this vacant place

Father

Just when I believed you did not matter

My delicate life began to shatter

Crumbling from the absence of your name

Marking me with limited fame

The loss of self; the denial of truth

Legacy of life belonging to you

He whom I derived my name

The man who has caused my constant pain

A Mother's Will

Yearning to create a lifelong legacy

Built on honesty, pride and prosperity

Uniquely divine in her pursuit

Moments of paternal truths

Negatively looked upon during her youth

Protecting her children at every whim

Acting as a life force for each of them

Caring, loving, and protective

A lioness watching over her cubs

The richness of a mother's love

Independence and Courage

Raw images of American ideals;

With Wordsworth and Whitman appeal

Stark resemblance to my father's kin

Like the masculinity of the Hudson

Pen-brushed and ink drawings will not last

Proceeding towards the future

Unmarked dreams

Capturing hope inside of an electrical beam

Dwelling within this quintessential existence

A hidden ounce of gloom

Centered on resistance

An exhausting and immediate defense

An exterior victory

Eased in religious faith

The greatest of strengths

Valued in weight

An Earthly Release

Within the presence of Darkness;

Susceptible to release

My spirit freely enters a calming peace

My soul embraces this meeting

Summer and winter sharing a kiss;

A brief friendship with death

Incarnated in life and time

Deathless attachment to my soul;

Curiosity and resentment accompany me

Into the stairwell of darkness,

I venture through

Fierceness of the night

It comforts my dying soul;

I delight in this calm release

And begin to let go

Descending into the dusk of evening light

Awaiting the judge of all judges to arrive;

For he is the final judgment

Sunlight falling around

My helpless spirit emerges

While Darkness escorts me

Into the deep of night;

My weakened human spirit

Bound to its soul

Acknowledging

What is gone is gone

Therefore, releasing me

From my earthly bond;

The allusion and delusion

Of Hell dismissed

A Final Kiss

His words drew blood from my lips

A bountiful and poisonous kiss

Sharp sounds of words enveloped

In the sweetest voice

Spoke the spirit of peace

The moving of thy lips ceased

Immortality awakened

A steady faith now shaken

Broken Dreams

His piercing blue eyes gazing at me

Equalization of a rare human being

Impatience waiting at every door

Preventing my dreams from being explored

Remote am I a blossoming dream

Restricted to this waterless stream

A well so dry it bares no fruit

Anguish and pain the ultimate truth

Inside my mind I contemplate

A life with you I refuse to erase

Too wrapped up in this ideal thought

Husband and wife the final result

I must admit too much time has past

Looking deep into this hourglass

Appreciating all which life has given me

I dare to hope for a blossoming dream

Pride and Prejudices

An internal feeling of deep pleasure

Wrapped neatly in innocence

A self-gratifying expense of the heart

Contentment crafted and sculpted;

By the hands of Michael Angelo

Preconception of ominous opinion

Absence of rhyme and reason

A state of conflicting affairs

Hindering compromise

Singularly impaired

Ordinary People

Human beings engaging in life

Contemplating truth in strife

Rising daily to an awakening call

Standing firmly among them all

Trying desperately to recognize self

In a world absent of wealth

Realizing that time has passed them by

Not really comprehending the reason why

A note to me in this sudden burst

The awkwardness of an internal thirst

The need to know who I am today

An ordinary man wasting my time away

The World in Which I Live

The grandeur of the day

The blue breath of the water

A relaxing spirit like no other

Springing into happiness

Flowers dancing freely in the wind

Men appreciating the human spirit

The magnitude of my life unhinged

Gripping my soul deep within

Forgiveness and Faithlessness

Today I seek forgiveness for all sins

A prayer from the fallen angel within

For all the wrong I and others have done

The hope of being forgiven by the Holy one

An entity of great power and faith

The one who has forgiven this human race

A race divine for its outrageous flaws

Contempt and corruption abound

Resisting the purpose of this sacred ground

A land unique with elements of life

Paying homage to erase all strife

Concerning to the naked eye

Observing and witnessing multiple lies

Untruths freely spoken by the average man

Requesting true forgiveness for the faithless

The Dawn

An internal awakening

Within the core of man's soul

Resentment towards his enemy and foe

A harsh and tragic reality

Too painful to let go

A pathetic excuse

Of one's overzealous ego

This reflection of self

Is often difficult to endure

Most complex evaluation

Of man which must be explored

To close the door on this hidden truth

Will cause great pain

Attacks on others who are not

Considered human beings

To deny this reality

Only perpetuates the cycle of hate

Ultimately leading to

Man's darkest and deadly fate

Time

Time waits for no man

Inescapable elements of life

Measured in seconds, hours, and days

Expiration of human life quickly fades away

Parting Waves

A high current came in

And parted waves

The current was so strong that

God could not stop the rift in the tide

For two years the direction of the wave

Changed on an unimaginable course

The waves while calm proved to be

Toxic and Tragic in nature

Those traveling along the path of the waves

Were oblivious to the outcome which

Was foretold by Abraham and Noah

This weathering storm is at present

An unbeatable element

Which filters through our lives

The Battle Within

Members of this unit

Have been killed or captured

Partisanship or Bi-partisanship

United and armed

Or divided and unarmed

Free of conspiracy

Or part of a conspiracy

The choice of man

Has never been so questionable

Difficult and challenging

In both respects

The Battle Within all of us must rest

This is a minor request

From a single voice

Military duty and patriotism

Often come to mind

Within these dark

And challenging times

Re-invention of self or destruction of others;

Not my brother

A slight misconception

Plaguing this great land

Divided we fall; together we stand

Holding hands will magnify our strength

Refusing to bond will demolish our race

A race of confused beings

Living in a state of isolation

The Battle is mighty

With its dangerous plight

This is a Battle in which

All of us must fight

We must fight for change,

Peace, dignity, and faith

We must do these things to save our race

Fragile are our thoughts

As we engage in this journey

The journey of a new world,

And an unknown result

Take fault in this current revolt

A reckoning which has emerged

In multiple assaults

This is no isolated incident

This is definitely "The Battle Within" us all

Every American who refuses to fall

A Silent Reprieve

Revolution, change, freedom, and democracy

An independence of self or country

Industry of heart or industry of mind

Conjecture refined

Oh, say can we see, from this obvious light

Of day change which has cloaked

Our citizenry

Marked on this blusterous,

Wintery day in May

Silence falls on our country's ears

Promoting unity or conspiring separation

A mild attempt of desperation

Omission or submission

Of voice

A Silent Reprieve;

No ones choice

The imperialist

Overzealous, quick temper, unruly, liar

Overbearing requests for more money

And power

Twitted repeatedly on the darkest hour

Discriminative notes

Trumping up charges against

All men, women, and children

Towering over masses of land

Striking a mighty blow with one hand

A grand stand; from

This dishonest man is unworthy

The votes, the followers,

The rallies, the views

An agenda focused on changing world views

CNN is the news

We reject the Imperialist

And his views

Weakening our moral fiber

And defying our hopes and dreams

What does all of this madness mean?

In a world of such uncertainty

American against American

Black against white

An unconscionable fight

A manmade plight

Constructed by the Imperialist

Absolute control of our great land

And our individual lives

This supporter of nationalism

And destroyer of civilization

He continues to rule in his own name

Meager attempt to confirm and promote

His worldwide fame

Someone who continues

To capitalize from the political stage

Obama

We loved him; we hated him

No one could ever debate with him

Some wanted to be like him

A man of dignity,

A man consumed with pride

A man who refused to lie

American pride

A symbol of hope,

Persistence and prosperity

Someone who demonstrated how

A President should be

Poised with grace, intellect, and humanity

Standing firm in his restraint

Representing what we ALL should be

Americans with faith, Americans with honor

American sisters and brothers

United under one flag

A country united under America's grace

One Bonded by a United Human Race

A politician confident in what he knew

Absence of Red and Blue

Reaffirming what most of us knew

A true Patriot

How blessed are we

To have witnessed his leadership

A testament to the greatest of depths

Truth in spirit, honesty, and trust

The guiding light for all of us

Locked in this cell

Cryptic to release us all

From an American Hell

A State of Confusion

There is a lack of understanding

Within this place

An unlimited depth

Of uncertainty rules these states

A sense of mutability

And indecision abounds

How distasteful this hesitation many witness

Classified merely as skepticism,

Doubt, or ignorance?

A rare dubiety

Yet, incertitude spikes

From all aspects in this life

The state of confusion

The state of a human plague

Bewildered or unclear

The utterances which bring forth fear

Perplexing; complicated plight

Discomfiture, devastation,

Daze, or just bamboozlement

Joe Bidden

Grip these reigns of national

And foreign policy

Be the political protector

You have chosen to be

Four and a half decades,

You have selected this plight

You have the opportunity now

To make all things right

Military engagement

In a never-ending war

Preeminent power near and far

Public service revolutionary and bland

America's future is in your hands

Captivated by duty, captivated by choice

Growth for America to ensure

Her prosperity and voice

From 2019 spanning to the coming years

Joe Bidden this is your time to lead here

Revitalize this economy

Shift our current state of existence

Renew America to confirm her stance

In-sourcing and outsourcing

Is our only chance

Global leadership; shifting power

Universal values overflowing

Core strength unknowing to any degree

Alliances and enemies fueled with envy

Partnerships as global as Europe

Foreign affairs

Unparallel in nature

A renewed consensus;

A new and improved presidency

The Bushes'

Be it family,

Duty or power

In this darkest hour

Intriguing and astounding

The Bushes' of Washington

Similar to Camelot;

A story of fortune or not

Conceptual views of plentitude

A family of seven

Mother, father, and child sent to Heaven

Tragedy

The Red Robin

The Washingtonian Texans

A mere suggestion

Aloof to the ideals

Of political royalty

From 41' to 43'

America embraces thee

Be it patriarch or matriarch;

A family set apart,

Competitiveness embodied

In heroism and faith

A sense of real grace

In a daunting place

Revelations of fear

Far and near

Which often reappeared

Historical statues;

Triumph and true

Dignitaries for a society

Of the red, white and blue

Enthusiasm amidst;

Challenges abound

Within this earthly crest

A Bush burning bright

On the dawn of night

Exemplary truth

From elderly to youth

A family strong

Remnants of a spiritual and holistic bond

An example of a dominant truth

Rapidly produced

Mother, father, sister,

And brothers; a united truce

John Mc Cain

American Aviator

Gliding in flight

Policy protector

Armed for the fight

Be it politics or warfare

John was there

Paying tribute to America

As her heir

Prisoner of war

A Republican;

Like never before

Once more, John was there

Fearless Lion

Roaming Capital Halls

The wilderness of this land

Held in his hand

Directed brilliantly

By this modest man

Arizonian true to his word

Committed to America

Like a red and blue bird

However You May Wish to Interpret Me

Since my existence,

You have been the sole provider in my life

You have been so since

The beginning of my life,

As you will be at my demise

You are rough to the touch

With your crinkling appearance

You are sharp and precise with meaning

You make it possible for

All my dreams to become a reality

So many depend upon your services,

Yet many have mistreated

Your existence of importance

I strongly appreciate your comforting me

When you are not in my life I feel afraid

Luckily, I can always acquire your services

Because without them I feel nervous,

I fear my every step

As long as you are in my life,

I shall not weep, nor shall I feel regret

Acknowledgements

I want to give thanks to my daughters Brooke and Brittney for being my role models for creativity. I would like to thank my cousins Jeremiah, Jermaine, and James for always encouraging me to do more with my life. To my sisters Barbara and Roshell, thank you both for listening to me over the years and making me laugh and sometimes sharing tears. That sister support is powerful. To my cousin Tonya who is inspirational in her own right. You are such a kind-hearted soul. Thanks to my son Michael, my niece Christina, and my cousin Jenatine for being such direct speakers in this world. Ralph and Regina, you two have always been a presence in my life. I want to thank my Aunt Rhonda and Uncle Cherokee for providing me with guidance throughout the course of my existence. Finally, thanks to my parents for giving me life.

ABOUT THE AUTHOR

Dr. Lisa R. Washington is an educator who works for the Baltimore City Public School System as an English Instructor. Teaching is her passion, and she truly enjoys working with students and helping them reach their full academic potential as young scholars. Throughout the course of her professional career, Dr. Washington has helped many students become creative and technical writers in addition to helping them increase their reading, speaking, and word knowledge and vocabulary skills. Many of her former students either attend high school, are enrolled in college, or they are career professionals. Dr. Washington is a certified Special Educator in addition to being a certified Reading Specialist. She is an avid reader, a gifted artist, and an impressive and talented writer. Poetry is her favorite genre. She enjoys teaching literature. Her favorite poets are Poe, Hughes, Frost, Dickinson, Blake, Angelou, and Whitman. Her published works include the following titles: *The Dawn of Time, A Quantitative Study on Student Engagement at Achieving the Dream and Non-Achieving the Dream Community Colleges Evaluated with CCSSE Data,* and *A Matter of Perspective: A Philosophical and Poetic View of Life, Death and Relationships.*

Made in the USA
Middletown, DE
21 May 2021